Little Kicker Country
where we live
ony the Pony's
lover patch
Emma Cow's mountain path
The Mountain
ond
Farmer John's
barn
atercress Patch
Sandy the Sow
Pig's mud hole
Daddy & Mother
Donkey's grazing
spot
Little Kicker's
kicking circle

To
Grayson
♡
Sandy Sprott
2018

A Book of Bible Based Values

A Prayer for Little Kicker

God has a special plan for my life.

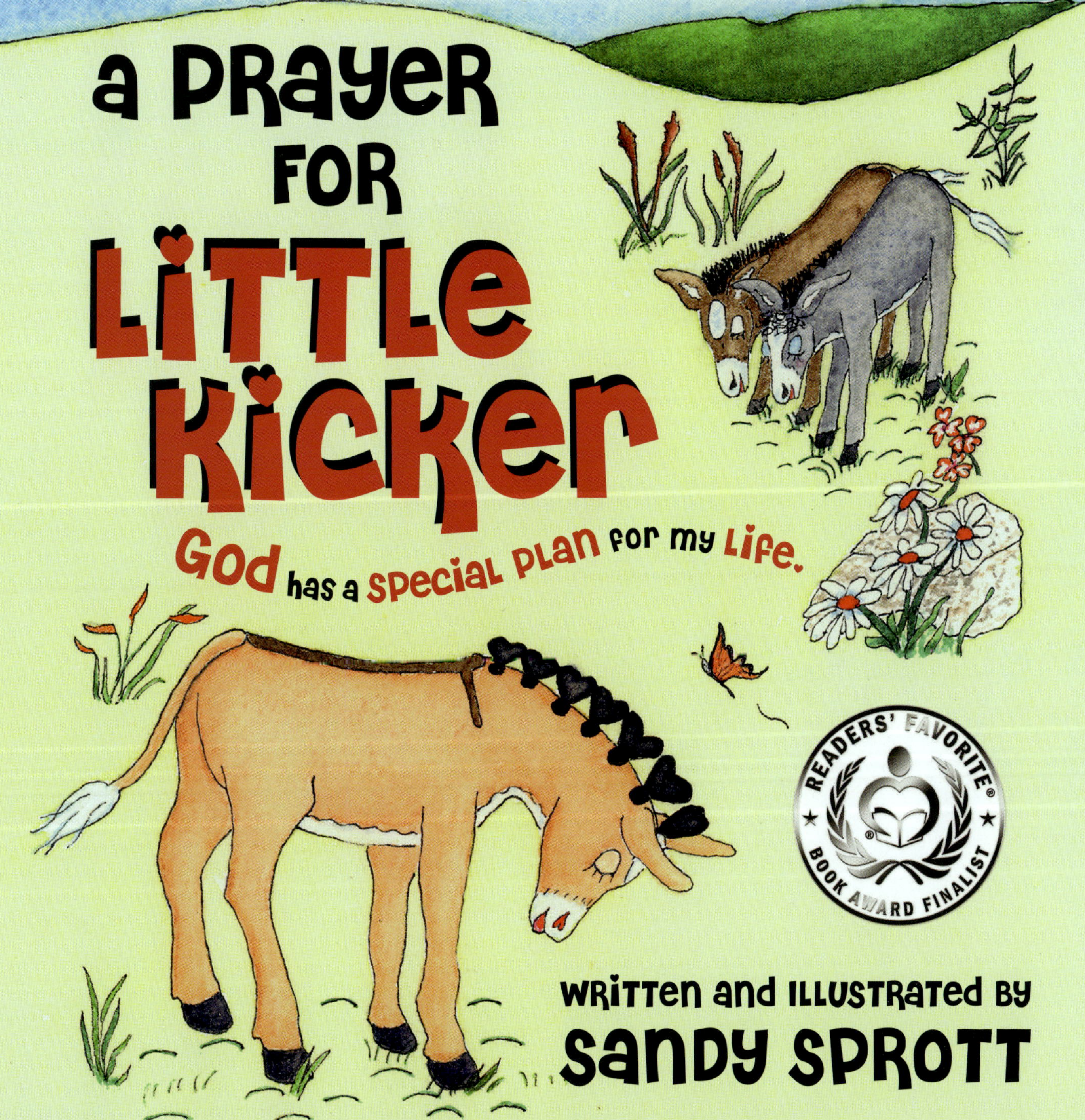

Written and Illustrated by

Sandy Sprott

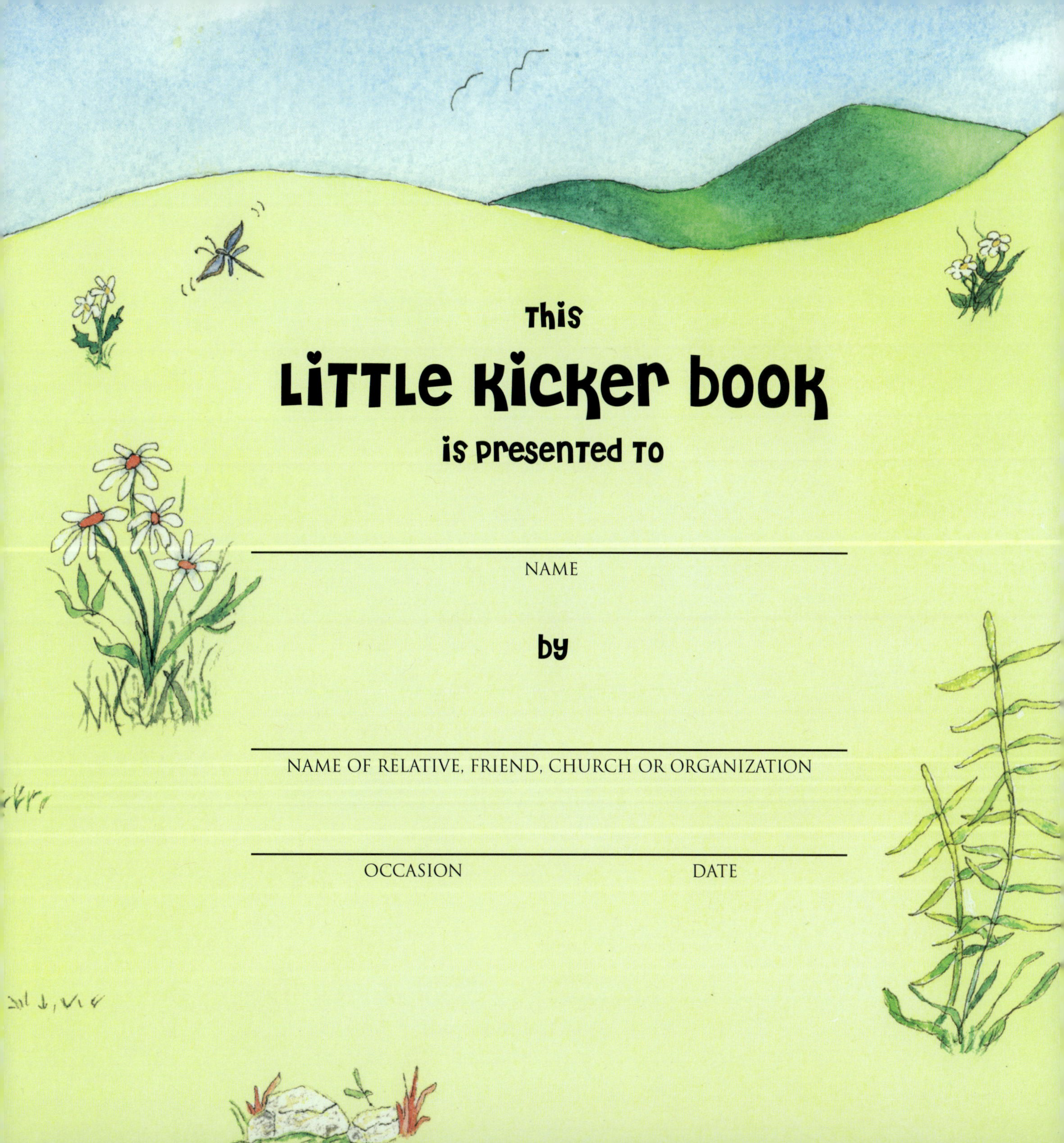

This

Little Kicker Book

is presented to

NAME

by

NAME OF RELATIVE, FRIEND, CHURCH OR ORGANIZATION

OCCASION DATE

A Prayer for Little Kicker

Published by Kimble Creek Press, www.KimbleCreekPress.com

Cover and text design by Diane King, dkingdesigner.com

Editing by Sam Sprott

Publisher's Cataloging-in-Publication data
Sprott, Sandy.
A prayer for little kicker / written and illustrated by Sandy Sprott.
p. cm.
ISBN 978-0-9843956-0-6 (Hardcover)
ISBN 978-0-9843956-1-3 (pbk.)
Summary: Family and friends of Little Kicker, a baby donkey, are excited to celebrate his birth and young life and welcome him to his home in the Ozarks. They pray that he will do something special for God someday.
[1. Donkeys –Fiction. 2. Ozarks, Lake of the (Mo.)--Fiction. 3. Prayer—Fiction.
4. Animal babies—Fiction. 5. Christian fiction.] I. Title.
PZ7.S7688 Pr 2011
[E]-dc22 2010910116

Manufactured by Color House Graphics, Inc., Grand Rapids, MI, USA
First Printing .... August 2011
Second Printing .... February 2013
Third Printing .... April 2015

www.LittleKicker.com

This book is dedicated to our firstborn, Becky, who has always loved books. As a child, you loved to wear hats like your Papa John. Thus, in this series of books about Little Kicker and Friends, you are Becky the Bunny. You delight everyone with your happy attitude and you have a hat for every occasion. Your father and I love you beyond the rim of time. Enjoy!

"Our Baby," said Mother Donkey proudly.

She and Daddy Donkey smiled lovingly as they looked down at Little Kicker.

Little Kicker was true to his name!

He kicked and bucked and tested his little legs from the very first day.

Mother and Daddy Donkey loved Little Kicker and watched him grow stronger each day. They loved God. They wanted Little Kicker to know God's love also.

"Let's bless Little Kicker," said Daddy Donkey. "Let's invite our friends of the field to come and pray for him."

Mother Donkey ran to tell Sandy the Sow Pig, Emma Cow, Rachael the Little Red Hen, Sam the Lamb, Becky the Bunny, Tony the Pony, and Tammy the Turtle. She asked them to come to the special day of prayer for Little Kicker.

Sandy the Sow Pig said, “Oink, oink! Of course we will come! All children are special to God!”

Everyone was excited. They wanted to pray for their new friend.

All the animals got ready. "We want to look our very best," they said.

Sandy the Sow Pig resisted rolling in the mud. Emma Cow polished her brass bell. Rachael the Little Red Hen cleaned, preened, and fluffed her pretty feathers.

Sam the Lamb washed his wool until it was as white as snow. Becky the Bunny put on her most favorite hat. Tony the Pony liked his new horseshoes, and Tammy the Turtle splashed in the pond to shine her shell.

Tammy the Turtle waved good-by. She must leave early because turtles walk very slowly.

All the animals gathered around Little Kicker to pray.

Emma Cow prayed, “Dear Father in Heaven, may Your Holy Spirit guide this special little donkey colt.”

Sandy the Sow Pig prayed, “Please, Lord, help Little Kicker do something special for You someday.”

Tony the Pony prayed, “May Little Kicker tell others about You, Lord, so they can know how wonderful You are.”

Sam the Lamb prayed, “Dear God, please let Little Kicker love Your Word, the Bible.”

Becky the Bunny prayed, “Dear Lord,
please help Little Kicker remember to
talk to You every day in prayer.”

Tammy the Turtle prayed, “Please help Little Kicker learn to do good things. Then he can help others.”

Rachael the Little Red Hen prayed,
"May Little Kicker always love You and
want to learn more about You, Lord."

Daddy Donkey prayed, "Dear Father in heaven, please answer all of these wonderful prayers for Little Kicker. Please keep him safe. May he do something special for You some day."

Mother and Daddy Donkey both said, "Amen."

Little Kicker had the sweetest smile on his little baby face.

Somehow, he knew this was a special moment in his young life.

God has a special plan for Little Kicker. I wonder what it is.

God has a special plan for you. I wonder what it is.

Would you like to have a special day of prayer just like Little Kicker?

Knowing God's love is an amazing thing! Maybe your friends and family would like to gather around and pray for you, too. You can grow up knowing the Lord, just like Little Kicker.

Special Prayers for me

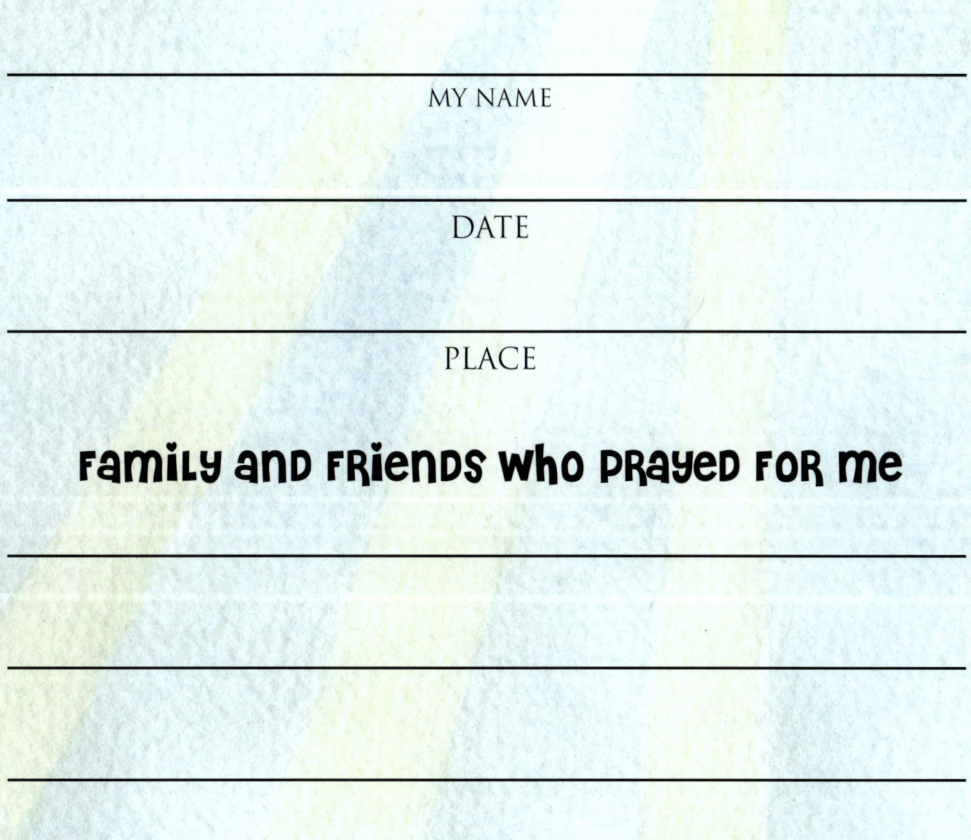

MY NAME

DATE

PLACE

Family and friends who prayed for me

about Little Kicker Country

Animals of the Ozark Mountain Region

Fun facts and insights for adults to learn and teach to children about God's creation and provision

Tree Frogs live mostly off the ground in bushes and trees near a water source. These cute little frogs have padded, suction-like toes that help them climb. I have seen them on windows of our home at night. Tree frogs are nocturnal and enjoy eating crickets and other small insects. It is pleasing to the soul to listen to them sing on long summer evenings.

Page 6

Page 6

Red Worms can grow to a length of five inches. Fishermen like to dig them up because they make great fish bait. Red worms feed on roots and plants that are rotting in the soil. They are valuable because they aerate and fertilize the soil. The bigger beige ring around the worm is called the saddle. The saddle aids in reproduction and may contain eggs. God made this worm a simple creature, but it has a big purpose in making our soil rich, healthy and productive.

Summer Tanager is a brilliant, colored bird. This one is a juvenile male. The adult is solid red. Tanagers eat bees and wasps and will even raid their nest. They catch many insects in mid air, but they also eat fruit and love peanut butter. We enjoy watching them from our back porch.

Page 7

Page 8

Toad Frogs eat many harmful insects. They are harmless and fun for children to catch and carry around. Some parents discourage children from doing this by telling them that they will get warts if they touch these frogs. The real reason parents say this is because when the frogs are picked up, they urinate as a defense mechanism. Most kids don't mind. They think it is funny, especially if it happens when they are showing the frog to their schoolteacher! Ha! Ha!

Box Turtles are a common sight in spring and early summer. They are often seen on roadways. Locals are fond of them and try to keep from running over them with their vehicles. Box turtles are harmless, and children may gently pick them up to view them more closely. A box turtle never has to run home for protection like a fox or a rabbit. Its home is on its back. When danger appears, the turtle tightly closes its shell and hides inside. To see if the danger has passed, the turtle will open its shell just enough to peek out. If all is clear, out come its head, tail, and four legs.

Page 10

Page 24

Chipmunks are ground dwelling rodents of the squirrel family that may grow up to a foot in length. They are cute when their cheeks are stuffed full with food. Chipmunks are a valuable part of God's plan. Their tunnels aerate the soil and slow the run off of rain. They even eat harmful insects plus insect larvae.

Fun Activities for Children

1. There are five tree frogs on page 6. Can you find them?
2. How many hearts are in Little Kicker's mane on page 25?
3. How many animals are on page 26? Do you remember their names?
4. On page 20, Becky the Bunny is praying. Name the animal crawling toward her.
5. Please find the numbers one through ten on the happy tree on page 12.
6. There are several hearts on Rachael the Little Red Hen on page 22. How many can you find?
7. There are six animals on pages 28 and 29. Can you find where each animal is in the story?

about the author

Sandy Sprott grew up on a 125 acre Ozark mountain farm.

Preeminent among Sandy's many and varied interests are her Lord, her family and her church.

For over forty years Sandy has ministered to children, Sunday School teachers and children's pastors at home and abroad.

It is Sandy's desire that this book brings comfort, purpose and delight to children.

exciting, award-winning

Little Kicker Books®

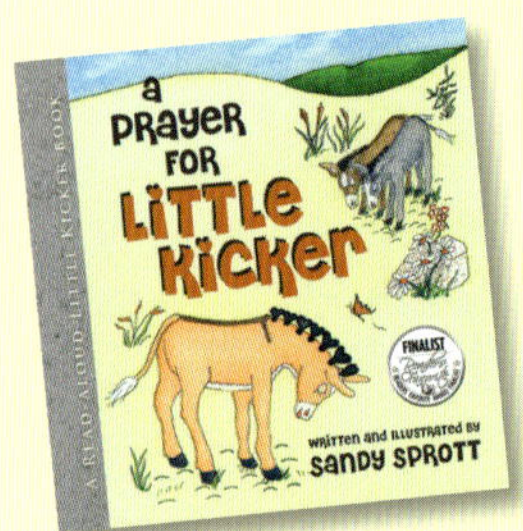

A Prayer For Little Kicker (Little Kicker is prayed for by family and friends.)

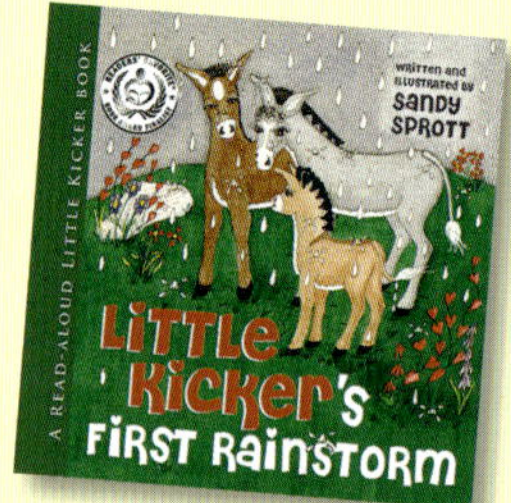

Little Kicker's First Rainstorm (Little Kicker is taught to pray to overcome his fears.)

Little Kicker Visits Doctor Quickwell (Little Kicker prays, and God sends an answer.)

Little Kicker Wants A Turn (Little Kicker asks for prayer to handle rejection when he is not chosen to play with his friends.)

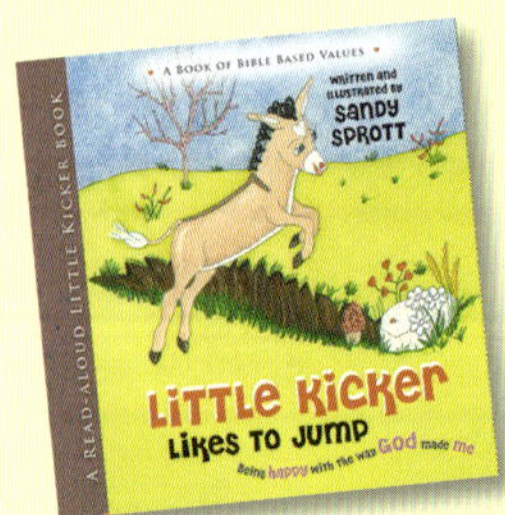

Little Kicker Likes To Jump (Little Kicker enjoys running and jumping. He is happy with the way God made him.)

NEXT A Chapter Book (The life of Little Kicker will continue in our first exciting chapter book. Little Kicker learns about creation and that it is never wrong to do the right thing.)

Coming soon!

www.littlekicker.com

www.facebook.com/littlekickerbooks

Through this book and the series of books to follow, Little Kicker faces trials as well as exciting adventures.

Little Kicker is a precious donkey colt that is new to the big, wide world. His parents want him to be able to do something special for God someday. They pray for Little Kicker that God will direct his young life.

Just as Little Kicker's parents prayed for him, we encourage all parents and guardians to pray for their children that someday they too will do something special for God. Your child may be used far beyond earthly expectations. Your child might be the instrument that God uses to turn the hearts of people back to Him.

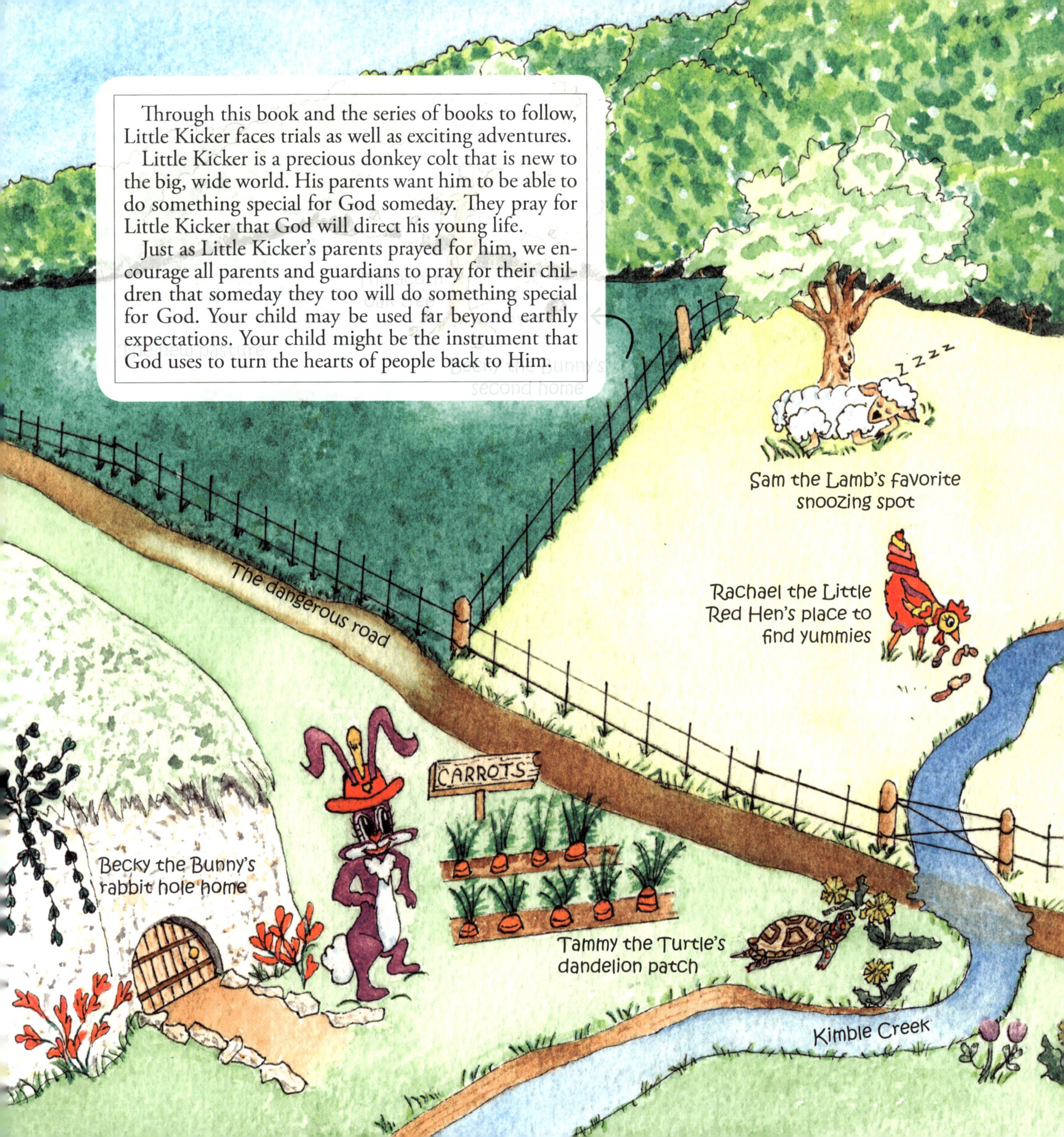